explanations

Poems and Essays by
Christopher Peyton Miller

RESOURCE *Publications* • Eugene, Oregon

Resource Publications
A division of Wipf and Stock Publishers
199 W 8th Ave, Suite 3
Eugene, OR 97401

Explanations
By Miller, Christopher Peyton
Copyright © 2005 by Miller, Christopher Peyton All rights reserved.
Softcover ISBN-13: 979-8-3852-1729-8
Hardcover ISBN-13: 979-8-3852-1730-4
eBook ISBN-13: 979-8-3852-1731-1
Publication date 2/15/2024
Previously published by Warwick House Publishing, 2005

In memory of my father, Rudy.

I thank my wife Kathy, my mother Joyce, my siblings, and my friends for believing in me when I did not do so myself. I have learned illness can be overcome through true relationships.

Contents

Animals	1
Baubo	2
The Blacklist	3
Deconstruct	4
don't cut me up	5
Driftwood	6
explanations	7
exteriority	8
A walk	9
for immortality	10
clouds	11
hind sight	12
hypnotic ride	13
nightsparrow	15
Tract on Obscuranti-Physicalism	17
reflexion	20
Sleepy rain	21
the end of physis	22
The Epic of Anihl	23
wondermania	30
worldviews	31
yielding	33
Disparity	34
Explanation	37
At the end of my rosary	40
The Cross of gold	41
Dig a Trench	42
Indulgence	43
writing Latch Key	45
Kedu Ben	47
Theodicy for the Sexually Abused	48
God, Process and Disparity	53
About the Author	59

Animals

they are not different, separate, above
see them scurry for morsels
grasping all, all grasping
climbing on each other

they snatch away the priceless and mundane
some kick, some bite, some smile
using there tools, extending themselves
encroaching, staking a claim, taking the same

their disgusting little features, little quirks
trying to be pleasant, modest, and tame
alone they grin, dreaming of the taste
their snarl, their penetrating eyes

with cunning and strength
they plan and seize
submission established by lies and loudness
organized thoughts and full threats

Baubo

I needed someone to get inside my head
I thought that they could know the inside through my language, I had this pain throughout my being
So I went in search of therapeuw
First I met with skinny Dr. Pavl
He said he could make me better with his formula
There is nothing on the inside and only acting on the outside. He said if I learned to pull the levers on his machine I would be okay.
But I still had terrible thoughts and feelings.
So I met with Dr. Cogito, who had a formula also
Feelings are not necessary set your
thinker straight.
So he twisted my discourse.
But pathos stayed,
My unthoughts were greater than his philosophy.
On my way I met a monkey
I said to myself he can't have what I have inside
I ask him "Do you know the way to Mr. Ant?"
The monkey pointed, I got lost.
That monkey lied to me.
While I was lost I found Master Zen
He suggested I be my pain, that's what I am
I'm not me, I'm not, so my pain is not.
I sat with squinted eyes, it gnawed at me.
So I finally went to Mr. Ant
He uttered semantikos
Then I helped him carry a larva back to his den.
He said the gnawing is in your hardwiring
Ants can really understand my unthought.

The Blacklist

Will, Oneness, Nature, Power, Freedom
Unity, Process, Purpose, Subject, Ultimate
Infinity, Object, Nothing, Universe

list

variousness, disparity, determinators
multiplicity, coyote

Deconstruct

deconstruct, deconstruct, deconstruct
what i construct is fabrication

deconstruct, deconstruct, deconstruct
from your gut, what you construct is contrived

deconstruct, deconstruct, deconstruct
necessity breeds deliberation

deconstruct, deconstruct, deconstruct
it's doubtful i can take any more

deconstruct, shut up, shut up
before all the pieces fly apart

The Blacklist

Will, Oneness, Nature, Power, Freedom
Unity, Process, Purpose, Subject, Ultimate
Infinity, Object, Nothing, Universe

list

variousness, disparity, determinators
multiplicity, coyote

Deconstruct

deconstruct, deconstruct, deconstruct
what i construct is fabrication

deconstruct, deconstruct, deconstruct
from your gut, what you construct is contrived

deconstruct, deconstruct, deconstruct
necessity breeds deliberation

deconstruct, deconstruct, deconstruct
it's doubtful i can take any more

deconstruct, shut up, shut up
before all the pieces fly apart

don't cut me up

don't cut me up
i don't have parts
i don't have a mind
i don't have a heart

your tongue is sharp
ready to explain
but i don't have a gut
and i don't have a brain

don't cut me up
leave me whole
for i don't have a spirit
and i don't have a soul

don't cut me up
i already said
i don't have an ego
i don't have an id

Driftwood

there is no gift
there is just driftwood
sticking to the bank
or slipping past a stone

with moss green
beads of water shimmering
each with silver outline
the water sifts

there is no gift
present and memories missed
not a flower sniffed
not even now, no gift

explanations

purpose has a dagger
whim has a sword
either way is empty
they're both just a word

they anthropomorphize anthropos
the tongue is guilty of betraying itself
they think what they say is directionality
they think what they do is intentionality

do they dominate
or are they infested with bugs
because they think they dominate
they think they can explain

if you listen closely at night
the ants will explain

exteriority

i am shudras
you have warned me
do not gaze at the sacred text
but you gaze at me

i use my implements
making death blows at theory
always with query
you look on, gaze

your intersubjectivity is...
exteriority
you do not see my suffering
eyes are only for the head they're in

you grasp at "psyche"
it eludes you
you construct
from your position

exteriority

A walk

glinting face that bronze that waste
brandy chewing candy to teeth like paste
the moment never disappears
it's clear cast dreams
through space through tear
drudge along in flight
kick gravel and always get
lost skirting off pace
is this how it will always be?

glinting face that bronze off pace and walking home
again brushing fingertips across rough edifice
meant much to one wondering
that glinting face that
builder of a kingdom in
this place and yet legs
brush together as fingers
trace smoke and candy an
ocean between is this how
it will always be?

delicate that face squinting eyes blink thrice
wet clothing hands intertwined
that bronze that waste oh to
escape the inward excursion
not a place or away that
sameness takes oh blinking
eyes and fingers waste is
this how it will always be?
Gravel skirting almost home now...

for immortality

if i hear it once again i'll scream
they say immortality's the thing
can't you see the limits of your skin
don't you know you are the bag you're in
the only motive or intent
is the feeling coming from the stint
just to feel your body twitch
just to scratch the primal itch
you may conceive it as you wish
but you're still no better than the fish
the look upon your face says fate
down deep inside you know it's fake

clouds

sitting looking at the patterns see the characters
children finding faces and animals in the clouds
these are the tendencies to create meaning
this is the beginning of the will labile latency
he said she said lavender thistle
sweet mint glorious dubiousness

privation of an urge, of an inkling
this is not a creation
there is no leaning here
inclinations and momentum skid
there is nothing inside the text

a pellet on the pallet changes the matter, the thought
ambiguity and i do not know who said this
loose leaf thoughts
the flesh is the memory
corporeal thinking

my gut is an empty vibrance
a reflection of the physical
the field, the blank from which comes nothing
i plant metaphysical trees so i can cut them down

the edges that can be, the distance i see
the edges of the body
infinity is the wish that i may become everything
everywhere, what do reptiles do with their time?

even sunyata draws on experience
what does the mite think of sunyata?
australopithicus aferensis trudging along like Sysiphus
adding and rearranging a world of myth for us

hind sight

just a wisp of a boy, and he kept mumbling, give me a break from the mind body problem, explaining everything, even the myth of myth, and how the numinous is flabbergasted, and is flagging wind torn, and he felt inadequacies halted.

how many times had he been told the stories, the archetypal shelters, through which the one, the many, and the empty seek refuge from the tumult, that grand production of flux, venting its formless harmony, that frightful glare that rises and falls, and his charm would embrace it for a moment.

bearing down with a flat pencil, leaving a trail of grey between a highway of green lines, not wondering of hereafter, or of a past, delving with tongue against teeth, a piece of flesh that would betray a faith, weeping and waning.

how ridiculous to believe there will be a great storm, and an end to it all, the composite of thought, temperament, permanence, it is all flagging in the wind, all hope reaches out to an entity, or entities, or something evolving from within.

plundering, all having been spoiled, taking in significance as though it were the last meal, that grub smeared all over each face, the gracious, the atoned, the enlightened, and all groan, and belch, and ask for more, while he sits scribbling those insignificant marks across the plane of a page, not an order of words, nor a finger pointing, nor the moon, and all those delicate phrases.

taking seriousness for granted, having it so many times, through the reference to heart, and the flimsy articulation of a mournful moment, though its gains are wavering, as they are seeking not the hindrance of his unflaunted predicament.

sitting on grandmother's lap, not a word said, without a warning guilt would come with such care, touching all places in a soul that is not there, that flagging and wind torn, hovering above, below, neither will do, not words, nor a finger, all significance weighs in each rigid moment.

hypnotic ride

hypnotic ride
so you want to be a part of my life
just take these splinters
and lay them side by side

everything is earthly
and not of any world
there is no rational to bow to
ideas and substance collide

and the lining is gold
but it does not last
the glow and the temperature
in a tilted hour glass

unsure of my very persistence
i didn't want to let go
dry mapped fingers hold on
how long will this moment last

it seems like an unhinged fate
this mire in which i participate
like a fly from place to place
the union of present and past

forgetting to oblivion
in a leap yet carrying on
a meadow of dandelion
a place and a road sign

steering disappeared
tracking lost its guide
connections were few and cool
on this hypnotic ride
language/body

in the infinite circularity
in the finality, all said
language strangles

the result, to resort
to submit to the pain
or enforce the same

there is another way
feel the felt rage
the dichotomous is failing
dance raving and railing

the tingling limbs
bust through the air
calves clenching
denying the nothingness there

thighs and gut revolting
epidermis molten
seeming eternal glows
in these convulsive throws

see not beyond the body
see not, it is declared
the entrenched is not entrenched
feel this indigenous ware

nightsparrow

winged at night and finally in that first flight. Then, hearing a "twiut twiut" chiding at dawn. Awaking from that territory long denied, lingering toward a mist-ringed light and being called back twice.

out in the morn, watching his rites, song, and flitter in a cold easterly wind, he labors to entice. oh, he does intend! little-ones'r his end. pushing clear song from a bold breast...above the usual stir of nature's business.

noting him for days. Only slightly warming is May's solitary air in which he is adept and forgotten. gathering grass and stems, pleasing his designer, with dedication.

he shows us his best, in vest, tie, and eagerness. fluffed and provocative above wanting nest. Between showers in June, and distances he flew. Prompt, poised, and gestures continue.

"Your flirtatious days outwit my dreams. Do you cause my unthought flight? And when stifling and tempest come, will you rest upon my sweating crown?"

creation has marked him out, unselected. Flying, having Dominion, remarkably pausing to take rest, to roost. splendid down of Three: ash, snow, and jet, impressive in simpleness. and attracting no mate yet.

to view with ease, to fully be. eternally in approach, perspective, and diving fearlessly. winged at night and finally in that first flight. he had made it to my dream, unwittingly.

lighting upon that neolithic greyness, four pillars vast and standing below a glowing mist. following, in flight above, that harkening to Oneness. swoop and then ascend toward wakefulness, and hear the sparrow chirping again.

I must go look at him sitting upon a fence railing. his call engenders a sad hope to awake in place and time. Impelled to worry over he who lingers, and fills in with flight the details of my nights.

Gliding, having Dominion, to view with ease, to be. a hero. Persevering not for destiny, but for the flitting of a wing. Over flesh, earth, and darkness I'm free, but through them I sing.

nightsparrow

winged at night and finally in that first flight. Then, hearing a "twiut twiut" chiding at dawn. Awaking from that territory long denied, lingering toward a mist-ringed light and being called back twice.

out in the morn, watching his rites, song, and flitter in a cold easterly wind, he labors to entice. oh, he does intend! little-ones'r his end. pushing clear song from a bold breast...above the usual stir of nature's business.

noting him for days. Only slightly warming is May's solitary air in which he is adept and forgotten. gathering grass and stems, pleasing his designer, with dedication.

he shows us his best, in vest, tie, and eagerness. fluffed and provocative above wanting nest. Between showers in June, and distances he flew. Prompt, poised, and gestures continue.

"Your flirtatious days outwit my dreams. Do you cause my unthought flight? And when stifling and tempest come, will you rest upon my sweating crown?"

creation has marked him out, unselected. Flying, having Dominion, remarkably pausing to take rest, to roost. splendid down of Three: ash, snow, and jet, impressive in simpleness. and attracting no mate yet.

to view with ease, to fully be. eternally in approach, perspective, and diving fearlessly. winged at night and finally in that first flight. he had made it to my dream, unwittingly.

lighting upon that neolithic greyness, four pillars vast and standing below a glowing mist. following, in flight above, that harkening to Oneness. swoop and then ascend toward wakefulness, and hear the sparrow chirping again.

I must go look at him sitting upon a fence railing. his call engenders a sad hope to awake in place and time. Impelled to worry over he who lingers, and fills in with flight the details of my nights.

Gliding, having Dominion, to view with ease, to be. a hero. Persevering not for destiny, but for the flitting of a wing. Over flesh, earth, and darkness I'm free, but through them I sing.

Tract on **Obscuranti-Physicalism**

1— The body is being, and vice-versa. There is nothing but vanity outside of bodily experience. Corporeality is more than Hume's sense experiences, and yet it is the same. Sensation, mentality, emotion, and the like are all proper to the body, and its privilege only. Subjectivity and objectivity are merged, and lose distinction in bodily experience.

2— The body is not a shell, and it is not divided from some soul. Soul and body should be expressed interchangeably, as should mind and body. Although we find no other choice language with its inaccuracy is the way we express experience. Bodily life is pre-verbal. It weighs in with significance like that found in pain and tickling. Elaine Scary's *The Body In Pain* is a good source of reading on bodily experience. Parts of Adam Phillips' *On Tickling and Being Bored* bring out the corporeality of experience, and should be read with an eye for the body.

3— Mind is illusive, an-atman hints at the nature of mind. Body is an ineffable tangibility. Mind is an illusive result, a resulting illusion, whose source is the body. Dennett is approximately correct when describing self as a center of gravity, or a meagerly and timidly informed consensus of the processes of the mind, which result from the activity of the brain. However, he would profit from emphasizing corporeality in his description.

4— Dualism reaches closure in the East, mind and body are seen as transitory. However, it is not preferable to think of the body as temporary. Temporality, time, is only a concept derived from the sensation of change. Being outside of time is the being of solidity, of tangibility, of the body. Change is a sensation, but the body is the basis of sensations. Though the body is subject to alteration, its physicality (its weight, significance within the world) lingers on. Some neurological patients have been known to lose the sensation of there bodies. But, they still exist as bodies producing limited, or different effects. Sensations, including mind, are not prior to the body.

#5— The word nature in #3 is not meant to imply unity within existence. Body (meaning also mental) experience is multiplicatus. The body is characterized by a weighty difference. The variety of bodily comings and goings does not suggest its emptiness. The reifying of emptiness can be leveled by a swift blow. There is a fleshy flow of experience. Numb heaviness, lightness, coarseness, and smoothness can all be in competition within the bodies repertoires.

#6— Consciousness, space, and emptiness succeed only where thought is given precedence. Consciousness sought in depth reveals emptiness, as Chopra affirms. He also finds emptiness within the great spaces of matter, which is given witness to by quantum theory. But the body is not matter, it is experience, tangibility. Again the body is not feeling or sensation but is being itself. The emptiness found in physics is grounded in data from instruments, supposedly extensions of the body, which are nonetheless alien to bodily experience.

#7— Body recognition of the groundlessness of knowledge is the experience of obscurity. Physicalism is not akin to materialism that assumes a definable structure to human interactions and being. The basis of which is activity in the world. The body does not manifest itself only in activity, but in inactivity, in felicitous and irrelevant agendas, in stumbles and divergent adventures. This bodily play is embedded with obscurity. Never a dull moment (generally speaking), but yet frequent dullness within its flux.

#8— On Hume. Passion precedes reason is an excellent description of mind. Passion is limbic, which paves the way for thought. More precisely limbic chemicals and cortex activity are inseparable.

#9— On Schopenhauer. Reifying will as Will suggests a structure of the universe. The competition, or play, of wills is primary to Will. Each will is bodily, when speaking of creatures. Bodies dance, wrestle, and plot.

#10— Much as Foucault speaks of the discontinuities of history, the body is laden with continuity and discontinuity. Discontinuity is more pronounced in some cases of trauma (especially neurotraumas) or illness. These can lead to fragmentation in conscious experience, which are the result of physical states. Obscurities in experiences both bodily and cognitively (which as attested is physical) can be recognized in "normal" bodies.

11— There is not time. Only bodies hurling, lunging, lugging through space. Time is how they are conceived, or felt even ever so distantly by other bodies. Time is how we sympathize with other bodies. Spirit or inspiration is a rush of blood, a palpitation, a chemical alteration that leaves one in awe. Soul and body, spirit and flesh originate from the concept of time too. Time is characterized as dual. The spirit is the wish to become, or the bodies forward inclination. On the other hand the body is disciplined for its having been, or its memory of itself. Memory is bodily and reflexive, which shows the bodies versatility.

Time and spirit are aspirations and devaluations of the body, and concepts derived from sensations. These show that the body is not always well intentioned toward itself. The body may castigate itself with its spirit. Sensations are seated in the body, but interpretations of them can lead to body disgust.

12— There is no unified unconscious, or self. Self is a concept which depends on the multiple risings of the shared lingerings of experiences. Or the body retains its interactions, an ultimate variety, which interact with each other, influencing each other, and always separate and combined. This is Deleuze's wolf pack in the work "A Thousand Plateaus." As for the self it is the bodies continuities.

13— Religion and psychology have been reluctant to "give the body its due." Why do we so often go beyond the body to explore the world? Science has sought unity. But experience leads us to discontinuities. We witness the compliance and competition of wills in nature. Why do we seek unity, instead of recognizing disparities? **Obscuranti-Physicalism** affirms experience that has been neglected. It sees a multitude of experiences with eye-balls, not the mind's eye.

reflexion

chronos collapsed upon himself
do you remember when?
And when, and when, and when
what a tangled nest
a mess
pull out a single strand, behest
it can't be done

sky fell in upon himself
glowings dim and bright
walled in
majesty been
and when, and when, and when
time and out of the blue
significance once true

earth buckled
her eschaton will swallow
always shaken ground
fall in and wallow
strata and folded terrain
sky earth time refrain

soma felt itself
it would not go away
closed eyes
and try, and try, and try
a cut would weep
warm ruby seep

Sleepy rain

sensations honor the augur of fretting leaves
heavy eyelids tempt to tuck away denuded fantasies
marbly drops sparsely bathe the dust-dry scape
each one its solemn voice upon the awning makes

bright beams suppressed by shady clouds aloft
dreams come of interest, the call of heart is soft
a glimpse of peace insets when day's nigh done
caring breezes fold around, then showers come

the end of physis

in a far land
where dust lingers
on expiring breath
the proclamation
"The end of physis is near"
blows throughout the hills
as each dusk weighs down
the whisper hits each new ear

arise, arise, you prophets
chavarka's star is burning
its dust is converting
its core is eternal
that speck, that particle

fail not the blessed reign
speak with your tired rasping voices
you see it as it is
give not way
plot those brains

up from the deep emptiness
that perpetual genesis
comes forth the monstrous consciousness
each molecule
creates the pool
from which it rises

The Epic of Anihl

Listen, let each syllable sear into the flesh of your brain,
the anesthetized slab that fulfills such fantasies as this.
Myth has an availing hold on the heart and its tuition.
So listen to the epic of Anihl, await the explanation of everything.
Shivering stood Anihl at the foot of the path, in the dark,
that naked place, only clothed by hands, and vibrations louder still.
Lo, many colors swarmed and took him in, curiosity and will.
A brilliant voice proclaimed, "Let there be darkness."
The incentive to fall to his knees besieged him upon the loam.
Anihl trembled and wept with shame, and only his own filth to claim,
having only begun to collect from the world he sought to own.
A light both distant and near caressed his fear into palpitation,
slowed and slowed, by that shouldering glow.
Anihl was given a lantern with a piece of the great light in it.
Many voices told him, as in Hymn, "Always carry this lantern
near thy breast, as warriors have in days past.
Its warmth will nourish thee, and give thee over
to greatest rest, oh great rest.
Thou wilst ever meet the great darkness, be thou alert.
With eyes peeled, for eternity thou wilst see the vastness,
and from all affliction will be healed."
Anihl began to wander and to wonder,
his path dimly illumined as he proceeded.
Darkness grew up on either side of him.
He heard the mumblings of beings, at the perimeter.
Though he felt a kinship to the creatures of the darkness,
he dared not reach out to them,
for fear that he would draw back without a limb.
His body be all he would ever know,
that which would be nearby, always.
"That night when darkness weighed upon my soul,
that aerial vestige would go, would go the companion, the hero,
covered not but realized 'twas never there."
Forbid that Anihl would ever be careless with such.
It disappeared instead, flew from his head,
which each night he lay feeling, and agreeing with its name, "skull."
Frightened by his own wit and morbidness, his sense of curiousness.
Imagining the contours felt by each fingertip.

" 'Tis this and this alone with which does exist.
No one with whom I meet can from me twist."
What follows is how Anihl lost, lost his soul, lost his light,
lost his way, but retained his dusty dignity.
"Oh dignity and breath that rising of the chest,
and weeping streams of beads, together threaded on soft cheeks,
how I long for thee, through tear, oh dignity, be only embodied here,
though I raise sword and nation, or sit still with imagination,
it all is given by thee and thy corporeality."
Thus spoke Anihl in a sigh of prayer.
Anihl's thick and laden heart gave up hollow songs,
hymns indeed to tame creatures.
Late one evening Anihl met a stranger,
who wore a plush robe with a very large hood.
Anihl noticed the large frontalis beneath the hood of the regalia,
and the inscription. Cumus mega philosiphicus, or something.
Lifting his lantern with his extensor digitorum
and momentarily away from his chest,
in order to better get the appearance of the robe,
Anihl felt a fire and a spooky coolness practically simultaneous
below his pectoralis. Gut feeling with its multitude of sensations,
never grounded and unified defied Anihl.
The stranger's robe indicated he was from a wiser place,
glaring red eyes betrayed this.
He invited our friend to illumine his path.
"Swing your lantern ahead of you, you are weak if and easy if
you do not penetrate into the darkness, give yourself over to
thought."
"Your heart is duplicitous, your head must lead the way,
and your gut must verify."
The stranger ended his speech with a grunt,
and thrust his fingers toward his gut.
Many times as a child in dreams and imagination
Anihl had come upon great robed ones.
They were always helpful and at worst benign.
"Division of head, heart, and gut," thought Anihl.
This somehow didn't seem likely, for the heart bleeds into the brain.
It is not clear whether Anihl first strayed.
Though the stranger's advice was well noted.
So our friend started down a path

with his lantern swinging out ahead of him, diligently.
Swinging the lamp brought a new turn in Anihl's moods,
able to see things once concealed. Grandiosity was evident.
He saw minuscule creatures of great detail, he poured over them.
He began to name each one, such a heavenly act for him.
Grasping them each two fisted.
Wringing them summarily and poking them under his hat,
a conqueror, emperor, god.
"Men have named us, let us not flee,
but serve in ignorance and grace our masters plea."
Anihl now had with an overwhelming vigilance,
tuned up to an anxiety, the need to secure.
These beautiful and awful creatures crawling and flying
as through cognition and dream.
"Poor Anihl" lay his lantern upon the ground,
firming knees and palms down and touching.
Unknowingly, Anihl feeling their tickling desperateness,
was using an inadequate approach.
Soon he had swarms of them dancing through his hair.
Anihl ran, panic, stinging ensued.
He ran upon a frothy and effulgent stream
at which he habitually knelt to wash himself.
The tickling continued well into his scalp,
and washing in the stream did not have an effect.
Anihl cupped water into his hands, onto his body
and began to rub it into his chest feverishly.
Exhausting himself with a neurotics bath, he collapsed.
In a vision of the stranger Anhil asked, "Mastema, is that you,
whom I dug up with a soup spoon in the dirt as a child?"
Dreaming? waking? seeing unusual things,
hearing disgusting laughter, Anihl met his foe.
Yes foe. Anihl beseeched the stranger, whose vast cranium,
now disrobed, gave no answer.
Their meeting was in the shallow water,
Anihl watched the stranger turn and walk away.
As the slight currents tickled Anihl's ankles,
he now noticed the stings from the creatures.
As he attempted to relieve the itching with a scratch,
Anihl noticed his frontalis was swollen.
The stinging was incessant, and caused much rage,

being alone no other knows the pain.
As he entered dwelling places, others placidly enjoyed their devotion,
he would scream.
Soon the lonesome path, the suffering excursion,
fraught with every diversion, yet empty,
and leaving one both worn out and excited,
he would reluctantly come to own. Shreak!
Looking around for his lantern, not finding it anywhere,
our protagonist began to cry out,
"oh lantern of my soul, my heart, once given in to thee,
I beseech thy whereabouts, I seek,
I do not want to be free, the glow once known to fill me
has fallen from my corporeality."
Darkness gave way to mist, grey, indifference
leading nowhere, states lower than emptiness.
The stinging, only numbness now,
thoughts grinding to a halt, creatures now amorphous.
Lips could not utter the vacuousness in Anihl's body,
not a stutter nor a groan nor wail.
Suddenly, a bolt, a search for more creatures,
as never known before, a calling, grand purpose.
The hollow chest remained,
but the cranium sought to be filled unendingly,
no thought was too great, Anihl would conquer, stand tall at the
finish, then ...there was no finish, no inclination.
Along his Way Anihl met a man in fine clothes, covering a sleekness,
who offered a sale. A lamp.
Poor Anihl had no capital to buy it with,
he had spent himself on his grand search.
As he began to walk along he began to wonder the most curious
thing. "Can I ever see where I am going if my feet cover each step?"
While looking downward, Anihl slipped...
Waking, stirring, feeling, fingers clearing eyes,
"I am upon a floor, firm yet giving way to,
something? Infinity.
Anihl lay on the floor of the abyss.
"That infernal capture of chained and unchained, I am He.
That serpent, that Creature of creatures, slithering,
causing unrest among the faithful. If not he, then akin!"
He searched for creatures to ingest. He found none.

Wo! How his body and head began to grow.
Little did he know, a battle was ensuing in him.
Soon Anihl's corporeality would fill the void,
evacuate the abyss, chase away the nothingness.
He heard Zarathustra's last squeak of a threat!
As his body pasted the prophet against the abyss.
Zarathustra was smothered by form,
not even to let out a Derridac yelp. Prophet with no body.
Anihl's empty body would become even a mountain.
He would create small creatures from clay, and breathe into them,
giving them movement. The wind from within him was full of
particles.
Anihl would touch the earth with his feet,
and the sky with the palms of his hands, "tactility!"
He became increasingly sad, though,
for his clay ones would not scurry about as he wished.
They instead sought to overtake him.
They swirled around their maker, causing universes.
Frightful places, for Anihl could only be in them with his thoughts.
"Tactility!" he thought.
At last he felt he had come upon a meaningful thought,
that would not devour his intent.
Then the sadness he dreaded came.
It had been long since that he had been with the lantern bearer.
Only Anihl's thoughts could carry him to the time
when he carried the lantern close to heart.
He feared that his body would remind him of such a time.
Tactility bent against itself, sorrow.
Lyrics began to play through his head. Or "was it demons laughing?"
"Spirit, reverence, stop!" Anihl began to mortify his flesh,
"be damned," "how dare I be reminded of such folly!" folly.
"I am greater than thee, oh mind, you weakling,
and your body inefficient, I cast nothingness to the Ground,
I am greater, you are my patsies,"
Knowing full well by which he was outdone,
Anihl was terminably sad, knowing only his body, alone.
His rage flew up, he could create All,
but he chose not to choose, not to move.
And he cursed every movement of his body, "still."
Head and chest heavy, increasingly difficult to breathe and to swallow.

Blacking out, "time."
Final darkness came,
Anihl found himself in an unbearably hot place.
Anihl despised heat.
Laughter, darkness, heat, more laughter.
This time the poor soul saw the source, "demons."
Flames charred, corporeality and tactility swallowed,
smothered in the heat.
Sweat in eyes, a familiar sting, "thought had caused this. Ignorance."
Anihl scrambled for answers, but, as before, nothing.
The demons impaled his sweet tactility.
"existing only as thought?"
He watched indeed that writhing on a stake.
Anihl had become nothing only to become something
and to be nothing again, a trace watching this sacrifice.
"A dream, let it be."
Out of body yet feeling pain, emptiness, punishment.
Anihl could not wake up. "Awakening!"
Could this go on forever?
Could the flurry that created forever reify its own production?
In a flash Anihl's body returned as it was before,
incarnated, fleshy, carnal dreams. "dreams?"
Where the body disappears, it only seems.
Giving cues to dreams. Giving clues to dreams.
Anihl only vaguely felt the twinges of torture.
Still hearing many voices, yet clearer, and saner.
"Many paths up the mountain."
Feeling tired from an incline he now treaded, he wiped his brow.
Our hero's cranium was beginning to envelope his eyes and ears.
His senses began to wane. He could only feel,
"Tactility, sweetness," he exclaimed.
But he could not make his way.
Living with no organization within he would soon yearn for a mind,
a path, seeking this or that.
At the end of the arduous incline,
Anihl stood upon the highest mountain. It was hollowed out.
A great form having hollowness.
Sitting on a far slope he saw seated figures,
repeating, "there is no mountain, oh weary fool,
you have tread upon yourself, you know, tricky footing."

Anihl understood the riddle, he was at once the seeker
and the sought, but could find neither.
Anihl would be punished or come to realize
the light he lost was himself. Great is Anihl's fate.
In either case he would suffer simply for being none other
than what he was, or was not. Fury!
Punishment would be more than dream.
And the loss had caused suffering only when he clung.
Anihl wondered if the punishment to come could be averted
by not clinging. He doubted it.
Trembling he fell onto the mountain, needing its salvation,
a glorious endurance not of himself.
Anihl clung to faith and then released.
He clung to self and then released.
He knew that neither clinging nor releasing had benefited him.
World and self denial face a lingering one.
That fleshy, supple, coarse, tingling body.
This is the manifestation Anihl came to know well.
For in that pit, that smoldering place, punishment was corporeal.
Fleeing the body in that place, was an indication of a dream.
Real punishment is embodied.
And enlightenment can only escape the sword by exoneration.
"One may be brimming with prajna, but a ball bat can free them of it."
The one lingering friend, the one who has the strength to forgive him,
is Anihl's own body.
Anihl must join the forgiveness, feeling the loss, the rage, the pain,
the remorse, digging in deep.
That beyond, that heavenly place, home of savior,
in this world and out of it, comes and is gone.
Anihl must only wait in his carnate place tending to wounds.

wondermania

wonderment, mania, pulses, and impulses
to soar, to be as no one before
brilliance, beaming ideations
reaching clearness

marvel more
and what's in store
mind outgrowing bounds
metathink, neurons blink
multiple fragments bent together
hashing out a billion processes
ineffable plans conceived

gladly welcome the overages flow
arrogance and secrets to know
unshaken confidence
cleverness in trance
fly o'er the precipice
a dancing exhibiting mind
endless facts to find

worldviews

the time is coming thanatos the secret is out
it kept rising up you would not be quiet
whisperings out of your sardonic face
all rising up was a deception of a deception
an illusion of a deception and still it came forth
                          though as a whisper
even when fear teeth clenched together lips pursed
                  neck stiffened but the whisper spurts
they will paint over you plaster you
they will build a structure for you
well carved intelligent hands crafting planing bolting
                        sustaining
            lifted skyward dropped through hell's hole
that gap gaping grasping from which you reach

reaching out to caress from threading stakes a flow chasing
                  down forearm trickle off elbow
you call out knowing full well language is a tinkering
                  weight of hand pushing even as written
you are not the one you are not one
            they are louder than your truth
regret and regression fill up with tension
there are many high places each experiences the weight
what strength it takes to speak from this
the world is in your mouth
            that gap gaping grasping from which you reach

for the fire to keep warming there must be consumption
speak out from the pit gap the flame they have you there
you can't see where you are going
stinging dry eyes from the extreme
more time taking apart the said live dead
nothing could stop the building of the structures
on which you suffer

you are for the spiraling outward

they are for the leveling off
all is sinking inward the mass has amassed
you gracefully linger out touching the tongue and the finger
they pin you down inserting insistently
all is spiraling spinning in on itself
dizzy heads throbbing craniums absorbed
once this all melts together will your structure
                      ever be in a fossil pose?

What is secretly known is that there is not one of you
but many throbbing hurting being pain in limb and gut
and experience
your crucible is erect filled with jet black empty fullness
left to glow in the night the vapid field on that hill
a veiny thrust in to rip out the contents it all will
be dissolved in a mixture of mud grey clay sediment rudiment
the basest element threat lived out; karma? no thank you, dead air

yielding

hoards of poor creatures
    prowling along all terrain
        balking, who's to blame

rid, rid unwanted dispossessed
    grow still from a swollen nest
       not contained

the yielding is extant
    a giving over in exhaustion
       truly never owned

too few eyes fell on the connections
      the hoards won't dissipate
        see heaven's Gate

Father adopts these incarnate spoil
      through their odorous pores' oil
        you must hold them close

in their glassy grey wintery eyes
    see not odd jealousy arise
       don't despise

Disparity

it is ineffable that science which delineates such transience
like putting on a hairshirt, fathoming disparity, despairing in trial
it once rose from the dirt measuring the affliction, meting out exactness
like a pungency which can flirt by wringing the meaning out of craving

it shall be ever sundered that mirror which is a mirage, a disguise
like a reflection of a blunder from which one cannot recover
it once gave weight to waiting notions of brilliances pure
like delving into flagrance or negligence without an hesitation

it cannot be at once an immanence of warmth and have a shredded essence
like a paling wintered divulgence letting by the glassy fire
it once rose up to salvage from defeat a nescient mewl floating upward
like timely fjords for tatters winding in this chink, this trace

it draws down gnarling what is stranded in its gestalt, which is ample
like an overlong machination leaning never toward belief in paltry penitence
it bares squishy any attempt to draw upon its fortune and depth
like the fickle tendon joining cognizance to credulity, oh innocence

it has always fallen but not abut, consigning us to such a lot
like an ogre's weight which when canceled leaves such an imprint
it is up to meagerness and yearning forthright to stall this bleak infiltration
like calculated verbiage and gathered deductions giving way to bodily curiosities

it offers a potion of cramp and ditty of what arises naturally from pith and ether
like the intangible onslaught whence presses forward clods and clay and corrupt extremities
it cannot be untangled that grimy remiss which dangles within each duration
like a gloom braved when the very fallible is stared at with deference

it is a shame that blankness summons such solemnity disclosing profanity in pantheon
like the innocuous eminence in the clenching engendered to each anguished fledgling
it is fraudulent to admit this clarity in a hollowness which folds into such a neat stash
like a forged calling does this hallowed bleakness yield such surety for the bumbling

when will the fullness come, the transcendence which flitters not nor falls?
it will be more than a rash dismissal of sentiment replaced with bulk and ceremony
when the sky literally cracks and glare jettisons the firmness which his heirs have buried
it has to swallow and permeate, leaving an effect mightily dwarfing its ill felt presence

when will the chronic tangibility crash upon the smug whispers of some non-duality ?
it is sure that such a stun would intimidate enlightenment into an untraceable distress
when will the sputtering and sabotage give out their tireless toss ever exhausted and drastic?
it is a feeling of clawing tactility, a trope of vagrant conviction smitten by each instinct

when the fulfillment is disclosed, the slipping between tear and glow will nag with regret
it will cost futile rage from which the complexity arose and the authentic impression fluxes
when any attempt at closure wanes, it is due to fear that barrenness will return in full swell
it is the collapse of chorus and lyrics which was the cradle and completion of this inanity

when the bidding results from that final scurry, will stupidity and frivolity cover grief ?

it is a tautology once disassembled giving logic for both its vulnerability and resurrected form
when glances come now it requires an ineptness that lingers through deadened limbs
it shall ever attract a somberness springing on an unwary and gruelingly suspicious savant

when all thoughts halt, and emotions still, to bring a state of unrelenting blessedness
it will be as a psychotic purge that jumps those who ignore its possible and unseemly result
when in spite of stilted arrogance the staggering event consumes with razing thickness
it is pitied that movement is vain without the relenting of this undesired reluctant mass

when giddiness requires dementia, where fury aims at the ground from which it flows
it is an oceanic incursion, which seeks to balance the very source of insolent waves
when will the regress to synchronous sensations come, the allure that animates the page
it will be that delicate fervor which embodies each sensation with its changing grace

when will the severity and dispute inflicted endlessly upon every inkling cease ?
it is a negligible slaughter of both intellect and tenor, a likely result of wretchedness
when comes the dreaded restoration by pity's graceful persuasion, chagrin
it will all seem a journey disguising itself as faltering calm and calamity

Multiplicity
Rhizomatics
Destruction
Eternal Recurrence
Divine self

Explanation

The poem Disparity refers to my religious experience, either what it was, is, or will be. and the science which is transience is how i always measure or evaluate my religion, lacking as it is. "hairshirt" in the poem is how i intentionally struggle with religion. a hairshirt is what ascetics like john of the cross put on to make themselves very uncomfortable. It rising up from the dirt is a creation reference, perhaps god's self creation. The "affliction" is the low state of grace it would find one in, the "exactness" is how living was laid out for me. A denial that any such experience was possible is found in how strongly that experience seemed to "wring" itself of meaning in the face of very human experience of "craving."

the mirror is the self reflecting the religious. not being able to "rise" from it is being forever influenced by it. there is probably some negative reference to resurrection there. After saying how heavy a "weight" the experience was, "delving" into it is "negligible," i admit the reference to "ledge" and "hurl" may be something about the suicide of the self that takes place in a religious-ascetic union with god, but "hurl" suggests puking, and nausea, kind of an extreme bodily negative to alleviate the spiritualization of the union.

the immanence of god, or the religious experience in general, is a warmth, but its very nature or essence is immediately realized to be flawed "shredded." there again may be a reference to the torn curtain in the temple at the time of the Crucifixion. the references to Christ are meant to put some disparity in Him, not seeing God as a unified reality. postmodern i suppose. "Wintered" suggests how drawn out this experience has been, it has been a "divulgence" an all-consuming one at that, the "fire" suggests warmth again, but only as an opposite of "wintered."

the mewl, or whimpering, is the state one is in before being rescued by the religious experience. being saved from the supposed emptiness and fleetingness of life, "chink" and "trace". Immediately again the religious experience is degraded as something which pulls down, "draws down gnarling," anything in its proximity. Next the "machination" is sort of a reference to determinism, which predisposes one to doubt, doubt that repenting will do any good. "squishy" suggests poor footing for those who seek to gain from spirituality.

there is a sense of consignment in the following lines. "verbiage" "deductions" and "bodily" makes an inclusion of spoken mental and bodily experience, making body the weightiest, but lightening it up with "curiosities." "Cramp and ditty" does the same, and "pith and ether" kind of a weird way to refer to body and spirit, hopefully to make the dichotomy look ridiculous. The two "cannot be untangled" within the religious experience. "Remiss" and "dangling" show the silliness of such a situation, "grimy" is how negatively such a situation would be seen by some.

a "solemn" experience exposes the absurdity "profanity" in the 'powers' that be "pantheon." "Clenching" is grasping for the religious. "Hollowness" seems to be equivalent to "clarity," obvious. "calling" again refers to some determinism, and "hollow" and "hallowed" play on each other.

and so the poem goes on and on ....until it starts to ask, when is this experience going to be something worth savoring, "when will the fullness come...?" my expectation is that it will be more than just ceremony and ritual but will "crack" the sky, here is a reference to the return of Christ on the clouds. the return will blow apart any attempts which have been made to refer to Jesus as merely mortal, hence the use of "burying" his "firmness" or godliness, maybe there is a similarity between the ideas of god, firmament, and "firmness."

"Tangibility" is a bodily experience that will "crash" on the Buddha "smug" "non-duality." There is a sort of anger directed here towards those who think that consciousness is the ground of everything. But directly back to the issue "when" will there be a relief of this kind of spiritual experience? Bodily experience seems to "claw" at even "vagrant conviction" even the silliest belief.   When the relief comes it is a hunch that the memory of this struggle will cause "regret" about how life could have been. even "rage" will have been in vain, it somehow shows the "complexity" of life. When it is realized that life cannot be simple truth experienced "when closure wanes," will depression's "barrenness" follow? The loss of joy "chorus and lyric" (the capacity to sing and write beautiful songs), was the "cradle and completion," the manifestation of this struggle "inanity." A reference to Christ as the Alpha "cradle" and Omega "completion."

Will i be this confused on my deathbed, in that "final scurry?" Taking truth "tautological truth" apart shows its "vulnerability" crucifixion and "resurrected form" resurrected body. Hope? "glances" of such truth come through the body "deadened limbs," "deadened" is there to offer a negation. "Somberness" will always be the approach to this matter for this idiot, it amusingly "springs" upon this dope every day. . . .Will salvation be as crazy as life has been? "will it be a psychotic purge?" Or am i being "arrogant" unthoughtful? "Thickness" "movement is vain" and "reluctant mass" seem to suggest a suffocation. Maybe the beginning of a real spiritual life will suffocate all this crazy debate.

the poem goes on and on....finally, "the giddiness requiring dementia" refers to the fact that i will have to become plain stupid to ever get back the joy ("giddiness" is a sarcastic way of saying "religious joy") that i once had. the first line in the last stanza refers to how every inkling toward religious experience i have is punished by my own doing. god may gracefully persuade me over time ("chagrin" "right" again sarcasm). will manic depression finally be seen as a preordained "journey" prepared by god?

At the end of my rosary

the overmen will overcome you
overcome your body
manipulate your body
"close your eyes and your body dissolves"
you killed him with your
mind his blood thinned with
water your finger prints
all over the sledge you
used his eternity has been
smashed his body and tears
so you went and bought a resting place for him for your dirt and sweat
fused to you as you uncovered that beautiful! But wait you were shoved
in or you fell in or you dived in but now clinging to climbing those
battered walls, many say "fall on your knees in penitence" others
"on your knees and deter grasping" those positions portray betray
each other, a thousand million times you could kneel earnest pure
and enlightened, and for reaching
out you had once been on
your knees feeling nothing
of your corporeality-real
and there you cried giving
honor and glory, but if you
were to fold your body thus
an endless storm of tears would
cloud you, oh! But to be lost
there. nirvana? shucks not
empty but full, full of rivaling
hymns conducted by discontinuity
thru the head the skull the cortex
flowing out tear ducts a rage of
chorus pent up, a revolution a
destruction a malfunction without
a part, loss of will if there ever is
ceaseless ambivalence which paints
colors in the dark in the chamber
of your head you see neurons for
what they are the emptiness
between you see, the fullness,
hear melodies and you see
your EmPtInEsS going
down down down
down down down

The Cross of gold

              will enlighten your path
though its reflection will not always be seen

At times in life It will stand behind you
but remember to look for its shadow before you
Its message may seem trivial to those about
but its old story can make courage of doubt

for days ahead you may wear it close to your heart
times will come when your closeness with it departs
you may PUT it AWAY IN your jewelry box for a SPELL
put it on often, remembering of WHOSE life it TELLS

Dig a Trench

Make a safe place for yourself
Be, man! Be!

Hesitation
Familiarity
Dig a Trench! Man!

"Don't you know how to Be?"
A Screaming, "No!"
Make a safe place, "Bunk"

making is for the makers
timidity shall inherit,
inherit eternity

"There is no time"
"You make this up
as we go along"

all fails the power of...
my name
let emptiness prevail

in this dark
silent
room

only the lulling
of the fans motor
my trench is dug

Re-Dig
Command, "Dig"
and dig some more…

Indulgence

Holding firmly to a thin branch, indulging
while slipping outward toward a twig

Having been before in a blank space, the depths
below only bring about indifference

The Fall, my fall, this fall
this is not a predicament, but
a state of becoming, yet not a
state, only a becoming

but why always to become into a pit?
"Thy ascendence is to the Right Hand
or below.... to the Tree"
and here we are on the branch again

Indulging, consuming Logos, producing
no goes, such nihility, no results, and praxis
fails, and thus the Fall, my fall, this fall
failure and frailty

'super' only in a world where fragility is esteemed
so go ahead break the branch, having ascended
for only a moment, fall and rise again
by the power of God or your bootstraps

the pit is not Gehenna, nor a field of
lavender, no blossoming lotus found here
Nor is it sunyata, just blatant blankness
a force, perhaps the Force of the universe

a shudder and a streak of lightning
some only have a glimpse, while others
fall, or rather dive in, headlong.
only the strong leap over, while others
fall to a depth of zero, nihil-nein-nicht

the factor playing here is credibility
"Do you believe?' "I am crucified
with Christ!" "Literally?" "Yes"
leaving behind this world of samsara
vacating, vanishing, extinguishing

"How boastful, do you save those
around you?" "Yes, when they follow"

writing Latch Key

Money is everything manna is everything
And I will dwell in the House of the Lord forever
foxes have their dens, all that is *to be had* is a trace
and from shame
I must move to Grace

THEY came and took my God away
or was it me? For shame, shame under
the trussel clear sky-air muddy water
and a passing that would take forever

yet here I am at thirty six and
return to that creek today, the
Russian history book I read at 16
is still on the shelf at the library
with *my name* on it

I've stood in lines of twisted futile
lives and seen what can be contrived
by vicious wolves and tame pups
poor and rich both wrench passing
on their heritage

not a solid mass of credence
nor to a palpable audience
cares and wishes are the meat for
them within four walls, housed,
and complacent

My Wish, to Cross a passing, eternal again
and again, yet only once, and it always happens,
I clutch and try to ride it out, it is my evil task
a Little quibbling in that surging eddy pus, that sore
collection of memories, which don't amount to much

when I am fully awake and it occurs to me

that the millions of leaves that live and die on a tree
pale in comparison to that which I see, in a day
or a decade, all but a nuisance to be in the extremes

Big E, little e, what begins with e? ear egg and elephant.
and is there a kingdom in a penciled drawing? Can one
ever increase on the glimpses of heaven and gehenna, forever
which are touched upon in memory, textuality, and curiosity

am I worthy of looking back, or pressing forward, or taming
myself? That ever increasing task of *solid*arity or *solitar*ity

writing Latch Key

Money is everything manna is everything
And I will dwell in the House of the Lord forever
foxes have their dens, all that is *to be had* is a trace
and from shame
I must move to Grace

THEY came and took my God away
or was it me? For shame, shame under
the trussel clear sky-air muddy water
and a passing that would take forever

yet here I am at thirty six and
return to that creek today, the
Russian history book I read at 16
is still on the shelf at the library
with *my name* on it

I've stood in lines of twisted futile
lives and seen what can be contrived
by vicious wolves and tame pups
poor and rich both wrench passing
on their heritage

not a solid mass of credence
nor to a palpable audience
cares and wishes are the meat for
them within four walls, housed,
and complacent

My Wish, to Cross a passing, eternal again
and again, yet only once, and it always happens,
I clutch and try to ride it out, it is my evil task
a Little quibbling in that surging eddy pus, that sore
collection of memories, which don't amount to much

when I am fully awake and it occurs to me

that the millions of leaves that live and die on a tree
pale in comparison to that which I see, in a day
or a decade, all but a nuisance to be in the extremes

Big E, little e, what begins with e? ear egg and elephant.
and is there a kingdom in a penciled drawing? Can one
ever increase on the glimpses of heaven and gehenna, forever
which are touched upon in memory, textuality, and curiosity

am I worthy of looking back, or pressing forward, or taming
myself? That ever increasing task of *solid*arity or *solitar*ity

Kedu Ben

Long ago in a primitive village, long before stories were written, lived the followers of the great hero Kedu Ben. He was known to vent his rage on those who honored him. He left many teachings, but the one that affects us today is the one concerning the end of what we know. The legend of the kedu bean. Of all his mighty and benevolent acts, only one threatened him. He once nearly choked on a kedu bean. He swore on that day (chant: kedu kedu ben) that he would return when the beans were ripe and would cause our village and the whole earth's population to simultaneously choke to death on kedu beans. Therefore, in honor of Kedu Ben, we must all swallow a kedu bean every evening.

This spread throughout the entire world. Every night before bed a kedu bean (or some other large bean, such as a lima bean) is placed into the mouth of even infants. All ages swallow the beans with no water. One hundred or so people die each year. As they gasp for air, the others mimic him and chant "kedu ben" and see the glory in his eyes as he expires. The dark period never mentioned by the kedu beners (only that kedu beners are meant to dominate the world) was when the armies of the kedu beners crammed beans down the throats of those who would not honor Kedu Ben.

What forms do kedu beners beliefs take when astronomers locate a meteor large enough to make life extinct? Things get crazy (people try to choke on beans) but eventually some obscure man, deranged as he is, is believed to be a prophet. He orders all to take their money they use to buy kedu beans and donate it to research. He can himself be the bean stalker, because he hunts the edges of the earth for beans to prevent them from being sold. There is quite a fight in congress between the bean sellers' enterprises and the bean stalker followers.

Eventually a laser is designed to shoot a ray at the meteor and knock it off its course. The meteor hits Pluto (keeper of Hades) and totally destroys it. Millions of people decide to tell their children that before the bean stalker kedu beners were persecuted. Their kedu beans were soaked in water and caused to swell up.

Theodicy for the Sexually Abused

Previously published in *Creative Transformation: Exploring the Growing Edge of Religious Life*. Vol. 5 No. 4 Claremont, CA Summer 1996.

To be a survivor of sexual abuse requires an unfathomable amount of determination and strength. A victim of sexual abuse lives with the memories of traumatic childhood experiences, which can trigger, at any time, an onslaught of negative thoughts and self-destructive behavior. One's sense of self-worth is continually bombarded by feelings of guilt, shame, anger and rage. Our society tends to blame the victims of sexual violence. Even those closest to the victim respond with blame and disbelief. Seeking out and maintaining healthy relationships for victims is usually the most dreaded and most difficult task in life.

A life of loneliness is often seen by the victim as more promising than continual pain and rejection in relationships. Victims of sexual abuse learn that the only ones they can trust are themselves (Woititz, 1985). Victims who choose to be alone in the world will often think of themselves as disgusting persons, unworthy of any attention. Making a connection with someone who can help is a step toward healing. But the only way for a victim to begin a process of change is to face the pain, and all the confusing feelings involved with the experience of abuse. This process works when it is done with someone who acknowledges and sympathizes with the abused. Can God be with them in their loneliness and pain?

What are the theological possibilities for the victim of sexual abuse? The following will focus on a theodicy that maintains God's relationship with the victim in view of the evil they have endured. The gender of God is important, for we know the majority of sex offenders are male. A male-oriented conception of God may be difficult for many victims to accept. However, a more fundamental problem exists in doing theodicy for the sexually abused. That is to find a theodicy that takes seriously the need for victims to see God as intimately involved in the process of healing their pain.

Classical theology conflates evil and purpose and ignores the felt aspect of evil. Traditionally, theology has been limited to understanding the problem of evil as "a logical problem which points to the logical compatibility of morally unjustifiable evil and the existence of an omni-benevolent, omnipotent, omniscient being" (Wachterhauser, 1985). The experiences of rage, pain, and confusion do not find a way into traditional theology. Let alone to find a connection between their pain and theology, the sexually abused will "explain away [their] history" (Woititz, 1989). Either they will deceive themselves or they will feel alienated by a distant God.

As a result many block out the reality of their own experience, which then prevails on an unconscious level and drives them into a life of self-destruction. Traditional theology has taught us "that feelings like anger and fear are not acceptable, and should be 'sublimated' or in some way not acknowledged or expressed" (Bowden). Survivors of sexual abuse already "hide their personal reality from others to avoid what they believe will be certain rejection" (Bowden, 1988). In addition they are encouraged to suppress feelings in the presence of God. A theology that encourages the sublimation of personal experience does not lead anyone into the fullness of life, instead into an uncontrollable life.

In a process theodicy, hope is initiated when one realizes God struggles with one's pain. God knows and experiences the evil that afflicts the victim. God feels the pain, knows the evil, and is yearning for the victim to have a healing experience. Hope for victims of sexual abuse comes when God is appreciated as feeling the feelings involved with traumatic experiences. "Human emotions are part of [one's] connection to God" (Bowden, 1988).

In process thought the fundamental datum for metaphysiscs is "nothing else but the experiencing subject" (Whitehead, 1929). The immanence of God is with every subjective experience. "God's causality is exercised in, through and with all other causes operating" (Mesle, 1988). God is intimately aware of all suffering. "Coming into an intimate relationship with the [victim] means hearing the depth of [their] pain, facing [their] terror, comforting [them] in the night" (Bass and Davis, 1988).

An omnipotent God feels no depth of pain or terror, therefore offers no comfort. But in process thought God experiences the depth of pain involved in sexual abuse, or any other human suffering. It is vital to understand that in process thought God is not power-oriented, controlling, or coercive.

One of the main objectives of process thought is to envision God working within "the tender elements in the world, which slowly and in quietness operate by love" (Whitehead, 1929). God does not force, coerce, or control, as a victimizer does. "God's influence is always persuasive and never coercive" (Mesle, 1988).

In order for a theodicy to be healing, God must be understood as being affected by and responsive to human suffering. In "every moment of the divine life God knows everything which is knowable at that time…God's concrete knowledge is dependent upon the decisions made by the worldly actualities" (Cobb and Griffin, 1976). Both God's knowledge and its corresponding emotional state are dependent upon actual experiences within the actual world. Therefore, God knows and feels the confusing feelings victims may have toward their abuser. God experiences the anger, guilt, hate, love, shame, fear and confusion. "Love in the fullest sense involves a sympathetic response to the loved one, sympathy means feeling the feelings of the others, hurting with the pains of the other, grieving with the grief, rejoicing with the joys" (Cobb and Griffin, 1976).

God loves the victim and initiates the hope necessary for the healing process by struggling with the pain and yearning for new and novel actualities. Since God's aim is novel experience, past, present and future are among God's concerns. God encourages the victim to confront the past and present, and to look forward to a future of novel experiences. "God is the factor in the universe which establishes what-is-not as relative to what-is, and lures the world toward new forms of realization" (Cobb and Griffin, 1976). God neither causes pain nor healing but provides the hope, the initial aim, for all new and potentially healing experiences.

A process theodicy has other practical aspects as well. When dealing with sexual abuse it is of the highest importance to have a clear picture of where the blame and responsibility lie. Each person has responsibility for her or his own self-creation even though God provides an initial aim, hope, and lure toward perfection. The sexual abuser's confused affection is their own creation, and they are responsible for changing their behavior. Hope for the abuser, and especially their victims, is that God "lures the world towards new forms of realization" (Cobb and Griffin, 1976). Responsibility for the destruction left by sexual abuse is not the victim's, but clearly the victimizer's.

God's activity in a suffering world is a lure toward healing and change. God yearns for the healing of the victim and change in the behavior of the victimizer. God's yearning provides hope. The weak will grow and feel the revelation and presence of God in their darkest moments. The strong will seek appropriate behavior.

God's self-disclosure comes as the revelation of the hope for healing. Victims and non-victims aid God's revelatory action when they provide opportunities for healing to flow from one actuality to another, from one's experience to another's. "Efforts to remove sin and suffering which help to obscure the divine love and lure may be the greater service to God's effort and self-disclosure" (Mesle, 1988). Support provides a context for healing, and thus the disclosure of God's activity. God is the God of relationship and connectedness. "Isolation is the worst of human sufferings" (Nouwen, 1972). A power-oriented conception installs God as one who knows no suffering and thus leaves the victim in isolation. In process thought God initiates the struggle with our painful past, creating hope and persuading us to create connections. The first phase of healing is to step into the dark past and meet God who feels your pain. "If to be free from the past were to exclude the past, the present would be vacuous. The power of the new is that it makes possible a greater inclusion of the elements of the past (Cobb and Griffin, 1976). God does not judge, blame, or incite shame. Victims can reach into their past and grasp the hand of God, who will gently lead them through the present and into the future.

References

Bass, Ellen and Davis, Laura. (1988). *The Courage to Heal: A Guide for Women Survivors of Child Sexual Abuse*. New York.

Bowden, Julie and Gravitz, Herbert (1988). G*enesis: Spirituality in the Recovering From Childhood Traumas*. Florida: Health Communications, Inc.

Cobb, John B. Jr. and Griffin, David Ray (1976). *Process Theology: An Introductory Exposition*. Philadelphia: Westminster Press.

Mesle, Robert (1988). "Does God Hide From Us? John Hick and Process Theology on Faith, Freedom and Theodicy," *International Journal of Philosophy and Religion*. 24.

Nouwen, Henri (1972). *The Wounded Healer*

Wachterhauser, Brice (1985). "The Problem of Evil and Moral Skepticism," *International Journal of Philosophy and Religion*. 17.

Whitehead, Alfred North (1929). *Process and Reality*. New York: The MacMillan Company.

Woititz, Janet (1985). *Struggle for Intimacy*. Florida: Health Communications, Inc.

Woititz, Janet (1989). *Healing Your Sexual Self*. Florida: Health Communications, Inc.

God, Process and Disparity

Previously published in *Creative Transformation: Exploring the Growing Edge of Religious Life*. Vol. 6 No. 3 Claremont, CA Spring 1997

> "The babble of inner voices produces *contradictions of will*, florid fantasies, the *spectra of viewpoints*, the conflict and choices; the inner babble means that we cannot understand ourselves . . . "
> (*italics added*) —James Hillman

Writing theology that captures the complexity of our imagination, which Hillman attests to, is a bold move. The critical task of bridging between the imaginal and the ideational is discussed in *Archetypal Process*, edited by David Ray Griffin. It would seem more difficult to write theologically in a way which manages to acknowledge the schizophrenic experience.

I realize the vulnerable nature of such a pursuit, and therefore approach it cautiously. My desire is to find theological language that does not stand in judgment of the mentally ill. I will attempt to maneuver in such a way as to uncover how God's grace is at work in process theology.

Whitehead's theological vision delineates God's lure toward complexity and interrelatedness. This vision of God is effective for the goal of recovery, which has been well established. While recovery is a momentous task, it is important to remember that some chronic symptoms may persist.

I suggest that some conceptual similarities with schizophrenic cognitive symptoms can be gleaned from process theology. These similarities may be valuable within the framework of a therapy that seeks to positively re-frame experiences. I agree with Michel Foucault who wrote that "nothing could be more false than the myth of madness as an illness that is unaware of itself."[1] Therefore, I am writing in opposition to pronouncements on schizophrenic experience which insinuate that it can be of no value or theological consequence.

Foucault hoped for a day when an attempt would be "made to study madness as an overall structure ...freed and disalienated, restored in some sense to its original language."[2] I feel that process theology can provide a context for complexity which can help in realizing this agenda. I can only offer a small contribution to this.

I believe that it should be established that God graciously accepts and enjoys some of the experiences of the mentally ill, yet yearns for a change in destructive experiences. I must point out my strong belief that illness is not equivalent to sin. With my motivations expressed I now will move on to show how process theology can recognize, affirm, and sympathize with some of the schizophrenic experience.

Whitehead speaks of going back to "that ultimate integral experience, unwarped by sophistication and theory."[3] The emphasis is on the subjective aim, not the objective claim. Whitehead's "integral experience" is the subjective, or felt, not the examined. Identifying 'experience' is essential to thinking theologically in a way that affirms the mentally ill.

Process theology realizes the interdependence of all things as they become, including mental and emotional experience. There is no separating, distancing, or estrangement. Whitehead speaks of interdependence when using the word society. He explains that " there is no society in isolation. Every society must be considered with its background of wider environment of actual entities".[4] Therefore mental illness is not excluded from having an influence on the world and God.

The schizophrenic's experience involves many thoughts contesting for the attention of the center of consciousness. There is no center, only a flood of ideas. It is as if they take " all possibilities into consideration, thus leading to a competition among incongruous and incompatible modes of response."[5] In process theology it is the competition of actualities which makes its impression on God.

The schizophrenic struggles with relevancy and irrelevancy, or over-inclusiveness. Whitehead wrote of God as the "actual entity in virtue of which the entire multiplicity of eternal objects obtains its graded relevance to each stage of concrescence."[6] Process theology envisions God as the conciliating factor between relevancy and irrelevancy. It would follow that God's experience abounds with contradiction and uncertainty, entertaining every possible actuality.

A universe where God is involved in even seemingly trifle actualities is reminiscent of a schizophrenic world view. Whitehead's expression 'novelty' describes how God could appreciate the experience of the mentally ill. Even 'delusions' gain relevance through God's initial aim. I must add that not all delusional experiences have destructive results.

In the schizophrenic thought process there is no ability to focus; there is a diffusion. A similarity can be found in process thought, in which reality is a stream which cannot be apprehended. In the words of Whitehead, "completeness is the perishing of immediacy: 'It never really is'."[7] Reality is not presumed to consist of separable stimuli, which are singularly grasped.

Some mental disturbances are characterized by a train of thought which has no apparent goal or purpose. 'Thought disorder' often includes an incessant use of illogical thinking. Diagnosing 'thought disorders' involves determining if a person thinks logically. "The demand for logocentric...syllogistic, logical, and noncontradictory 'thinking' is a prejudice adopted naively from Aristotle and the tradition of Western metaphysics, which to be sure, makes the same demands on thought."[8]

Associating God with disorder runs contrary to traditional theology. In a prophetic vein Whitehead warned that even science and logic would sooner or later arrive at contradictions. This has been emphasized by postmodernism, and has brought rationally based philosophy into crisis.

Another 'symptom' of 'thought disorder' is the preoccupation with immediate sensory experience. This might cause problems in a practical world full of demanding changes, but it is not devalued by process thought. Whitehead praised William James for his sensitivity to the present and his protest against dismissing immediate experience in the interest of system. Process thought acknowledges the past and the future as manifest in the present.

Immediacy is valued in its disclosing of the very nature of reality as process. The immediate continually slips away. "There is no nature apart from transition, and there is no transition apart from temporal duration. This is the reason why the notion of an instant of time, conceived as a primary simple fact, is nonsense."[9] Preoccupation with immediacy is a means to realizing that everything is in process, a delving into the very fluid nature of reality.

Where schizophrenia may find another connection with process theology is through the very experience of disparity in thoughts. Any theology that deals with such an experience of disconnection must confront and include this difficulty. 'Tangential', 'discontinuous', and 'disordered' thinking are included and validated within process theology. Whitehead stated that "the complexity of the world must be included in the answer."[10]

Where can the mentally ill find blessing in process theology? God can be envisioned as their contentment within their actual experience of discontinuity. "An actual entity is a process in the course of which many operations with incomplete subjective unity terminate in a complete unity of operation, termed 'satisfaction'."[11] Whitehead expressed the world of actualities as a diversity of events which reach their fulfillment only in their contribution to the next stage of possibilities. Such possibilities certainly would open the way for recovery. Expanding on God's initial aim would be an expression of hope. With an inclusiveness of thought and experience process offers possibilities for the development of theological notions which are compatible with the impressions and experiences of the mentally ill.

Can theological thinking be content with such disparity? I think so. I feel that process theology can offer a positive re-framing of experience which traditionally lacks a theological voice. The first step toward this move is realizing that "psychologically we (all) have many claims made on us from a deep place. It is not possible, nor is it desirable, to get these impulses together in a single focus."[12]

Creativity and beauty come to mind when we discuss the many places inside of us that contribute to who we become. This is definitely a theme of process theology. I think that in the case of schizophrenia process theology can help us see ourselves in others.

I began this essay with a quote from James Hillman that can leave an unresolved feeling about the very nature of our souls. Process theology emphasizes the indefiniteness and flux of our existence. Some approaches to psychology seek normalization. Any incongruity and incompleteness in expression are referred to as dysfunctional. The poignancy and novelty of life as it becomes is often missed. I feel it should be admitted that much can be learned about the psyche from 'florid psychotic states', in the end they are referred to as abnormal.[13]

Process sees no dysfunction in life, but the interaction of aims. These aims are not seen within an eternal plan (completeness) of God, but seen aside an effected God and world within eternal movement. Complexity is compatible with process theology, which validates the experiences of the mentally ill.

Whitehead taught that God's aim is initial in each life and in the concrescence of each experience. God's aim is seen aside other aims. The conflict of aims that is part of the experience of schizophrenia, when seen beside other lives, is extraordinary (to use Hillman's word) not deviant. I think that process theology can help us recognize this exceptionalness.

I have only begun to elaborate on the experiences of the mentally ill. There are experiences of catatonia, depression, anxiety and others. I admit that there are manifestations of certain illnesses that do not lead to greater complexity and interrelatedness. These are the major themes of process theology that would be the likeliest criteria for determining stages of recovery.

Nonetheless, my goal here was to express theological notions which affirm the mentally ill. Tolerance toward differing experiences is crucial for such theological thinking. This means valuing personal experience, even when it is unconventional. Process theology presents a suitable framework for reaching this goal.

End Notes

[1] Michel Foucault, *Mental Illness and Psychology*, (Harper and Row, 1987), p. 45.

[2] Ibid. p. 76.

[3] Alfred North Whitehead, *Process and Reality*, (MacMillan Company, 1929), p. 526.

[4] Ibid. p. 138.

[5] Louis A. Sass, *Madness and Modernism*, (Basic Books, 1992), p. 215.

[6] Whitehead, *Process and Reality*, p. 248.

[7] Ibid. p. 130.

[8] Irene E. Harvey, "Schizophrenia and Metaphysics: Analyzing the DSM III," in *Pathologies of the Modern Self*, (New York University Press, 1987), edited by David M. Levin, p. 316.

[9] Whitehead, *Modes of Thought*, (MacMillan Company, 1938), p. 207.

[10] Whitehead, *Process and Reality*, p.519.

[11] Ibid. p.335.

[12] Thomas Moore, *Care of the Soul*, (Harper Collins, 1992), p.66.

[13] Murray Stein, "From Freud to Jung and Beyond: Turning Points in Psychoanalytic and Religious Thought," in *The Fires of Desire: Erotic Energies and the Religious Quest* (Crossroad Publishing Company, 1992), edited by Fredrica R. Halligan and Robert L. Moore, p.35.

About the Author

Chris Miller is a graduate of Anderson University and received a Master's Degree from Hollins University. He is previously published in *Creative Transformation*, Center for Process and Faith, Claremont, California.

Chris grew up in Vinton, Virginia, where he spent many hours dreaming and contemplating other worlds. He was interested in American and Russian history as a teen. He has studied classical Hebrew and Koine Greek and is interested in Christianity and Eastern Religions. He presently resides in Troutville, Virginia, with his wife Kathy.

www.ingramcontent.com/pod-product-compliance
Lightning Source LLC
LaVergne TN
LVHW051710080426
835511LV00017B/2843